SOUTHERN ELECTRICS SCRAPBOOK
Volume I

David Brown & Kevin Derrick

Strathwood

First published 2020
ISBN 978-1-913390-67-9

Published by Strathwood, 4 Shuttleworth Road, Elm Farm Industrial Estate,
Bedford, MK41 0EP Tel: 01234 328792
www.strathwood.co.uk

The Southern Electric Group, founded when the pre-war main line stock was in its final days, celebrates its fiftieth anniversary in 2020. and the authors would like to thank members, past and present, who encouraged interest in the subject from the time when David participated in his first rail tour, the legendary '2-BIL Farewell', in early 1970 whilst Kevin watched it from the lineside. We are grateful to all those individuals and organisations who have provided access to their photographic collections for this volume; some real gems have been uncovered. Mention must also be of John Atkinson's 'Blood and Custard' website and associated Facebook group, which has been a treasure trove of detailed information to help bring the captions alive.

Finally, and sadly, during 2020 two important and prolific photographers of the Southern Electric, James Aston and John Scrace, have passed away. We would therefore wish to dedicate this volume to their memory.

David Brown, Chichester.
Kevin Derrick, Inverness.

Contents

Page

Opposite: This beautifully composed photograph of the most famous Southern electric train of all in a classic location was taken in the summer of 1971. In glorious evening light, 5-BEL unit 3052 leads the 19.00 Victoria – Brighton 'Brighton Belle' all-Pullman service passing Merstham on the Quarry line avoiding Redhill. Although the traditional umber and cream livery has given way to British Rail blue and grey, with their table lamps and oval lavatory windows the ten Cars are still unmistakably Pullmans. *Chris Wilson Collection*

Atmospheric Electrics

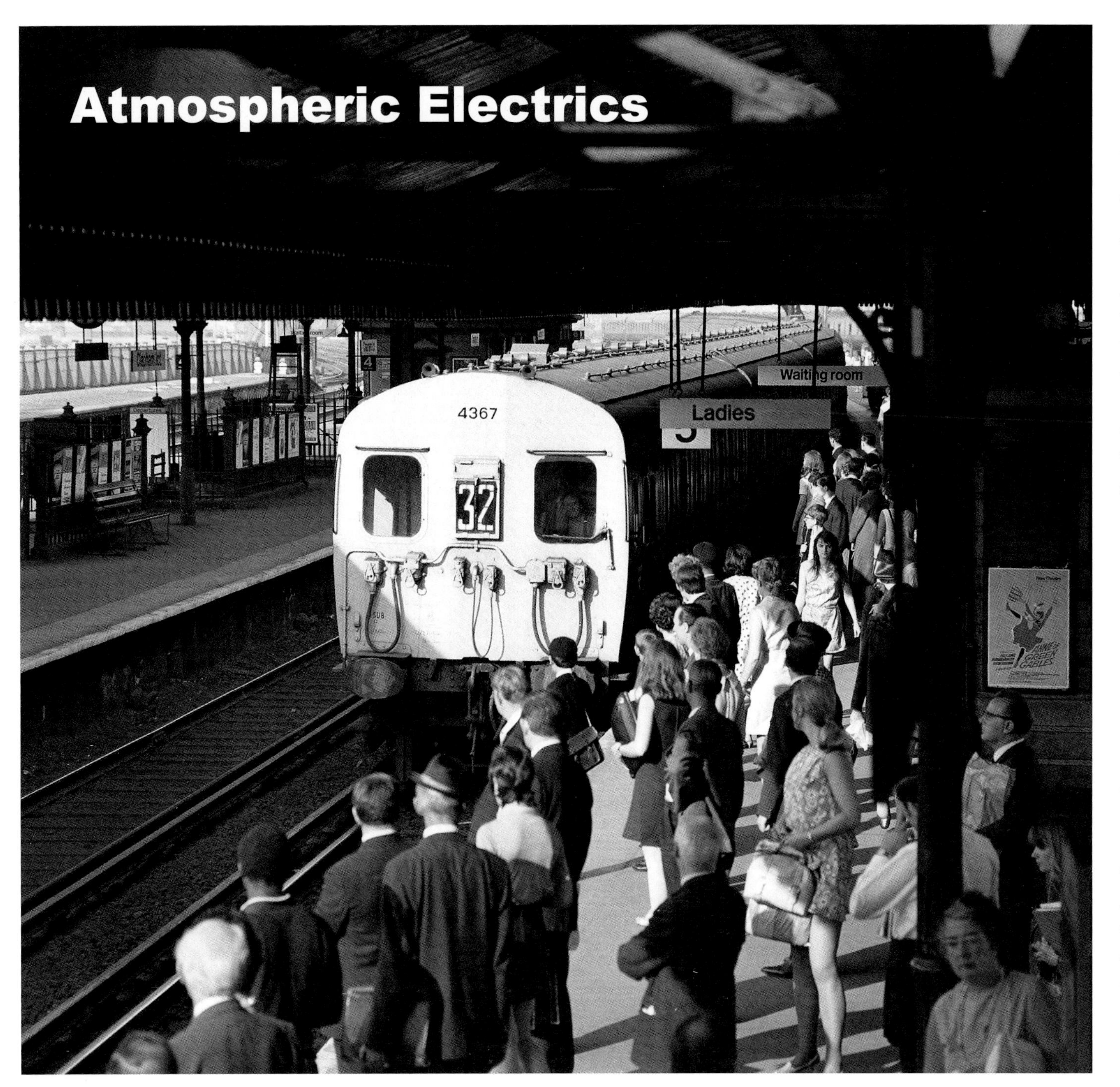

Left: Expectant home-going commuters pack platform 9 at Clapham Junction as 4-SUB unit 4367 runs in with a clockwise Kingston 'roundabout' service back to Waterloo via Earlsfield and Richmond in August 1969. 4367 was one of the relatively few 'all-steel' SUBs with all seating in closed compartments and the fierce 'eyebrowed' appearance resulted from handrails being fitted around the cab windscreens. These, and the step-plates above the buffers, were needed to change the headcode as the offside windscreen didn't open.
Brian Stephenson

Opposite: Here is a familiar scene which gradually disappeared with the introduction of electric starting bells on new stock from 1951 onwards. The Guard waves his green flag before smartly stepping into back into his brake van as a 2 BIL + 2 HAL formation is about to depart from platform 3 at Barnham with a service towards Brighton on 24 March 1969. ***John H Bird/www.anistr.com***

WAITING ROOM
PLATFORM
3
WAY
AND TRAINS TO
BOGNOR REGIS
PORTSMOUTH
2

42

Seen from the deserted down island platform, 4-VEP unit 7792, in its original overall blue livery with yellow ends, passes Ford on a murky day in January 1970 with a Victoria service. A 2-HAL, recognisable by its radiused windows and inset driver's door, stands in the down loop with the Littlehampton shuttle. On another very cold and damp January day in 1970, 'Sheba' 4-SUB 4106 calls at Vauxhall, platform 2, with a Chessington South – Waterloo service. At this time, the station platforms still carried a complete array of green signage. The ten 'Sheba' 4-SUBs were introduced between 1941 and 1945 and were the first S.R. electric units to squeeze six passengers across each compartment. The name originates from a Bible quotation concerning the Queen of Sheba who came with a 'very great train'. ***Both: John H. Bird/www.anistr.com***

Left: The mist rising from the Thames partially obscures the Houses of Parliament as, a few seconds later, 4-SUB 4661 approaches on the down fast line with a Waterloo – Guildford via Cobham service which will run non-stop as far out as Surbiton. It was quite unusual to see 4-SUBs on this route, which had mainly been the preserve of EPB stock since the early 1950s.
John H Bird/www.anistr.com

Opposite: 4-CEP 7173 is unusually diagrammed for a Brighton – Portsmouth service as it approaches Ford, while the 2-HAL standing in the down loop will depart shortly with a Littlehampton service. In this March 1970 view, a comprehensive array of warning signage of Southern Railway origin is evident attached to the signal post.
John H Bird/www.anistr.com

FORD
FORD
DANGER
DON'T TOUCH
CONDUCTOR RAILS
NO EXIT
WAY OUT
THROUGH
SUBWAY
PASSENGERS
MUST NOT CROSS
THE LINE HERE

After some initial teething troubles, Bournemouth line electric services with their unusual mode of operation had bedded down to reasonably reliable working by March 1968. In that month 4-TC trailer unit 410, propelled thus far by push-pull fitted B.R.C.W. Type 3 diesel D6580, runs into Bournemouth from Weymouth and is about to couple to another 4-TC and a 4-REP electric unit already waiting in the platform for the run to Waterloo. D6580 was the first of the class to be equipped for multiple unit operation with suitable electric stock, an important feature of the 1967 Bournemouth electrification scheme. ***John H. Bird/www.anistr.com***

Opposite: Seen from the station footbridge, this panoramic view of the London end of Clapham Junction dates from August 1966. Unit 4366, another all-compartment 4-SUB, runs into platform 11 with an evening rush hour Waterloo – Effingham Junction service. Apart from the depressing array of new flats, the skyline also includes the chimneys of Battersea power station. The overhead 'A' signal box, which came into use in 1912 and was re-equipped in 1937, controls the South Western side of the station while the post-war 'B' box controls the Central lines. ***Brian Stephenson***

4366
16
Way out
Buses
Shopping Centre
Platforms 1-10, 13-17
11

On the foggy New Year's Day of 1969, 5-BEL 3051 has just passed Keymer Junction and approaches Wivelsfield with the 12.45 Brighton – Victoria 'Brighton Belle', still in traditional Pullman livery but with a small yellow warning panel obliterating the crest on the cab end. Some minor track maintenance is taking place but, of the gangers, only the lookout man is wearing an orange vest. ***John H. Bird/www.anistr.com***

Opposite: : With her 1968 British Rail paintwork by now looking rather tired, 5-BEL 3052 draws the attention of an onlooker as it prepares to depart from Brighton with the 12.45 'Brighton Belle' service to Victoria on 18 March 1972, just six weeks before the retirement of this once prestigious service. Behind, a 4-COR unit in platform 2 will form a west coast service to Hove and beyond. ***Colour Rail***

Brighton
BRIGHTON BELLE
4

A glimpse through the ticket barrier to platform 7 at Brighton reveals an unusual visitor in the form of 4-TC 422 (powered by D6529) forming the Southern Counties Touring Society 'South Eastern Rambler' rail tour on 22 October 1967. The tour had arrived from London Bridge via the Mid-Kent line and Uckfield and would do a return trip down the freight-only Kemp Town branch before heading off towards Eastbourne. *Strathwood Library Collection*

This animated scene from about 1970 shows the ticket barrier to platform 16 at Victoria just prior to the departure of the 11.00 'Brighton Belle', with 5-BEL 3051 nearest the buffers. Special finger boards were provided for the 'Belle'; if you did not want to pay the supplement, you waited for a later train. ***Bluebell Museum Archive***

Above: 4-REP 3004, leading a pair of 4-TC units, pulls into Brockenhurst with the 15.23 Bournemouth – Waterloo service on 2 June 1967. In the down platform is another REP + TC formation pausing with a Bournemouth bound service, while in the up loop a pair of 2-HAPs waits. Modernisation had not spread everywhere; although the Bournemouth electrification scheme was virtually up and running, the station porter is still wheeling an antediluvian luggage trolley. ***John H. Bird/www.anistr.com***

Right: Chichester station was rebuilt in the late 1950s in a similar contemporary style to Kent Coast stations such as Folkestone Central. Luggage is being loaded into the brake van of 4-CEP 7147 as it calls with a Portsmouth Harbour – Victoria via Dorking service on 24 March 1969. ***John H. Bird/www.anistr.com***

Right: The 4-EPBs were a development of the all-steel 4-SUBs and were built in quantity through the 1950s, utilising the underframes and bogies of pre-war suburban stock. This study of a cab end from unit 5148 at London Bridge on 12 September 1956 demonstrates some of the differences. The buckeye coupler and waist-level hoses made coupling and uncoupling possible entirely from platform-level, while the sliding cab windows made the cab less draughty and headcode roller-blinds did not drop off en-route. The nearside power jumper and associated horizontal conduit across the front were found unnecessary and a source of unreliability, however, and did not last long.
Alan A. Jackson/Chris Wilson Collection

5-BEL 3052 was outshopped in the special 'Pullman' version of B.R. blue/grey livery with some vestigial white lining in December 1968, but initially retained her stencil headcode panel. Dappled by morning shadows in the cutting, she is seen here passing the remains of the closed New Wandsworth freight yard and approaching Clapham Junction as she nears journey's end with 09.40 Brighton – Victoria 'Brighton Belle' service in the summer of 1969. The lucky breakfasters on board should just be putting their knives and forks together. ***Brian Stephenson***

Unit 2950 was one of only three 4-LAVs to gain full yellow ends and was also one of the last of its class to survive. On 1 January 1969 it is seen emerging from the mist after calling at Wivelsfield, and approaches Keymer Junction with the 11.49 Victoria – Brighton stopping service. 2950 had its final day in traffic six weeks later and was scrapped in Chesterfield the following September. ***John H. Bird/www.anistr.com***

The bridges spanning the cutting make an interesting backdrop and the deep canopies throw shadows around the train as S.R.-bodied 2-HAP 5602 runs into Winchester leading a morning Bournemouth - Waterloo stopping service in August 1967. These units were built on the reclaimed 62ft underframes of scrapped 2-NOL vehicles and were therefore given Bulleid-style bodywork. The driving trailer composite is leading, showing the corridor side which is similar but not identical to post-war 'all-steel' 2-HALs. The station has recently been re-signed in the new B.R. corporate image for the Bournemouth electrification. ***Colour Rail***

Opposite: On a not-uncommon visit of its class to the coast, 4-SUB 4727 passes a fine S.R. junction signal near Ford, mounted on a post fabricated from old rails, while forming a Brighton – Bognor Regis service on 30 March 1969. Without a 2-BIL or HAL on the rear there will be no first class accommodation or lavatory facilities. The raised lineside cables on short concrete posts, and boxed-in with timber boarding, were a familiar feature of the 1932-39 coastal and outer-suburban electrification schemes. ***John H. Bird/www.anistr.com***

4727
31

Signal Check

The lines out of Waterloo were re-equipped with multiple-aspect colour light signalling in 1937 in readiness for the Portsmouth electrification. 4-COR 3103, built for that scheme, leads a COR + BUF + COR passing Vauxhall with a Waterloo – Portsmouth Harbour express in 1964. It has been fitted with roller-blind headcode panels but retains its whistle and has recently gained a yellow warning patch on its gangway. Due to their 'one-eyed' appearance resulting from the offset headcode panel, these units were generally known to railwaymen as 'Nelson stock'. *Chris Wilson Collection*

Opposite: 4-CEP 7122 leads an evening peak London Bridge – Littlehampton service at Portslade on an unrecorded date in the summer of 1965. Although at this time their main use on the Central Section was Mid-Sussex line services via Horsham, CEPs and BEPs regularly appeared elsewhere and in this case were possibly covering for late delivery of CIG and BIG stock. The signal post is again fabricated from worn-out rails and the traditional L.B.S.C.R. station signal box may be glimpsed through the open goods shed. *Chris Wilson Collection*

17

Displaying letter headcode 'L', vintage 4-SUB unit 4517 passes Wimbledon Signal Works with a Chessington South – Waterloo service on 21 June 1958. The unit pictured here was the second SUB to carry this number and was one of a series of twenty units, numbered 4501-20, formed between July 1956 and January 1957 as a stop-gap to allow the London-area 2-NOLs to be withdrawn earlier than originally intended. They comprised almost exclusively vehicles of L.B.S.C.R. A.C. 'Overhead Electric' origin, although two (4501 and 4511) also contained L.S.W.R coaches. The reasons these coaches were retained after other wooden-bodied SUB vehicles had been scrapped was firstly that they were among the youngest and secondly that their underframes – lengthened from A.C. vehicles - were unsuitable for re-use under new EPB coaches. 4517 was withdrawn eighteen months later, by which time 2-EPBs 5651-84 were in service to replace the NOLs (and indeed were built on the underframes of their predecessors). *Chris Wilson Collection*

Opposite: When the Bournemouth line was electrified the existing semaphore signalling in the Southampton area was initially retained. The gantry at the western end of St Denys forms an impressive backdrop as type JB electro-diesel E6007, the first of its sub-class and then almost new, accelerates through the station with the 08.58 Bournemouth - Waterloo service on 17 June 1967. The Mk 1 brake second behind the locomotive is one of the earliest Southern Region blue/grey repaints and the Gresley buffet car in the formation has been borrowed from the Eastern Region while the S.R.s own catering vehicles are in works being incorporated into 4-REP electric units. *John H. Bird/www.anistr.com*

CARTA
CARNA
WITH MEAT
95

This fine LBSCR starter signal has just been pulled off for the departure of 4-CORs 3151 and 3153 from platform 4 at Horsted Keynes with the empty stock of a rambler's excursion from Victoria via Haywards Heath on a winter's morning in 1957. The eight-car train will be a challenge for the limited power supply. In pre-Bluebell Railway days this branch was always incredibly quiet, pupils from nearby Ardingly College and walkers providing virtually the only traffic. In days gone by the area to the left had been filled with stored locomotives, coaches and goods vehicles awaiting works attention at Brighton or Lancing, but by this date the sidings had been cleared. ***Fred Ivey***

Still in green but by now sporting full yellow ends, 2-BIL 2026 runs into East Croydon leading an afternoon Victoria – Gatwick Airport – Horsham – Littlehampton service on 7 March 1969. Both vehicles of these units possessed side corridors connecting all compartments to toilet facilities. The four-aspect colour light signal dates from the 1955 re-signalling in the Croydon area while, for now, the redundant water column provides a convenient location for the 12-car stop indication. ***Chris Wilson Collection***

Passing under the signal gantry's in the shallow cutting where the Brighton main line out of Victoria crosses Wandsworth Common, 5-BEL 3052 leads the 11.00 down 'Brighton Belle' non-stop service on 15 September 1963. Although carrying the traditional Pullman livery, the crests on the front and sides are the elongated version adopted for the 1960 'Blue Pullman' sets for the Western & London Midland Regions and the new East Coast Main Line Pullman cars. The lineside photographers are waiting for a steam special to the Bluebell Railway hauled by Caledonian Single 123 and L.S.W.R. T9 120. ***Chris Wilson Collection***

Opposite: Some precarious signal maintenance appears to be taking place as 4-COR 3156 eases 'wrong line' down the up fast line at New Malden, leading a COR+RES+COR formation on a Waterloo – Portsmouth Harbour fast service. Onlookers standing on the footpath bridge behind seem to be showing interest in these Sunday engineering work diversions which took place on 29 May 1960. 3156 was the first of three additional 4-COR units formed in 1946 using spare motor coaches, left over following wartime damage, and new trailers. ***Dr Terry Gough/The Transport Library***

8
CAR
WA.47
TELEPHONE
3156
80
3156
6

2-BIL 2020, from the first production batch originally built for the 1937 Portsmouth and Alton electrification, is framed by signals as it arrives at Alton with a service from Waterloo in about 1962. By this time in the unit's late middle age, it is carrying the second British Railways plain green livery with carriage roundels. The Maunsell vans in the left background remind us that parcels and newspaper traffic was still ubiquitous on the railway at this date, often requiring stabling at various locations in between usage. ***Chris Wilson Collection***

Opposite: The fine set of semaphore signals at the eastern end of Ford station is again prominent as 2-BIL 2115 calls with a Portsmouth Harbour – Brighton service in about 1968.The driving trailer composite is leading and the large windows on the corridor side, reaching to the eaves in the distinctive style adopted by S.R. C.M.E. Richard Maunsell, are particularly well-illustrated in this view. Unit 2115 was withdrawn in October 1969, still carrying the livery shown, and was scrapped at Chesterfield the following March. ***John Vaughan/Chris Wilson Collection***

WAY OUT
TICKET OFFICE
& ENQUIRIES
TICKET OFFICE
FOR ALL TRAINS
ENQUIRIES PARCELS
AND LEFT LUGGAGE
2115
62

7109
52
7109

Opposite: 4-CEP 7109 leads a CEP+BEP+CEP formation passing Wandsworth Common with the 9.45am Victoria – Eastbourne/Ore express on 26 May 1963. It has clearly recently been outshopped and was one of the first to carry the U.I.C. yellow stripes to indicate first class accommodation. CEPs from the main production batches for the Kent Coast (7105 upwards) were not usual on Central Section services at this time and it was probably providing maintenance cover. ***Brian Stephenson***

Right: 4-COR(N) 3067 leads an unidentified 4-PUL unit into Brighton with an E.C.S. working from Lovers Walk depot in January 1964. Formed in that month from redundant 4-RES units by replacing the restaurant car with either a former 6-PAN trailer second or 6-PUL Pullman composite, these units had a short life and were further reformed into additional 4-COR units two years later. The train is framed by colour-light signals installed as part of the 1933 Brighton electrification scheme. ***Chris Wilson Collection***

From the start of 1964, 4-CEP and BEP stock displaced CORs and BUFs from Mid-Sussex line expresses. In March 1969 unit 7170, by now in blue and grey, approaches Ford leading a Victoria – Portsmouth Harbour/Bognor Regis via Dorking service and is again framed by the comprehensive array of semaphore signals and the box controlling them. At Barnham, the train will split, with the front portion running to Chichester and Portsmouth and the rear, including the buffet car, to Bognor Regis. ***John H. Bird/www.anistr.com***

4-LAV 2942 runs into platform 5 at East Croydon with a Victoria – Brighton via Redhill stopping service in 1965. Introduced in 1932, the LAVs were synonymous with the Brighton line until the last was taken out of service in February 1969. Seating was mainly in closed compartments as in contemporary suburban stock, but one coach had a side corridor with toilets at each end, hence the designation. Yellow first class cantrail stripes have recently been applied but not, as yet, a yellow warning panel. ***Chris Wilson Collection***

Lewes was an important junction station, as evidenced by the proliferation of signals at the east end. 20001, the first of the three Bulleid/Raworth Co-Co 'booster' electric locomotives, was at the very end of its career when used on 'The Sussex Venturer Railtour' on 4 January 1969. It is being well photographed as it backs on to the tour coaches prior to taking them on to Hastings via the direct Stone Cross chord avoiding Eastbourne, being the very last train over this section. The tour had arrived at Lewes from Tunbridge Wells West via Uckfield behind KA Type 3 diesel 6565. ***Chris Wilson Collection***

Opposite: The trees are bare and football matches are taking place on Wandsworth Common as another pair of 4-LAV units, with 2951 leading, pass under the two signal gantries with the 11.47 Victoria – Brighton via Redhill stopping service on 14 February 1965. It has yet to gain either first class stripes or warning panels. The flat-sided brake vans on the LAVs were a feature borrowed from contemporary Maunsell S.R. steam stock but were not repeated in later types of electric unit. ***Brian Stephenson***

2951
14

Type JB Bo-Bo electro-diesel E6022 stands at Southampton Ocean Liner Terminal after arrival with a boat train from Waterloo in 1967. Over the unelectrified dock lines from Northam Junction it would have been working at 600hp from its auxiliary diesel generator. The huge terminal in 'moderne' style was opened in 1950 to serve the largest liners, but by 1967 its use had diminished with the rise of long-distance air travel.
John H. Bird/www.anistr.com

Opposite: Recently outshopped in the new blue livery and immaculately turned out by Stewarts Lane depot, Class 71 type HA 'booster' Bo-Bo electric locomotive E5004 arrives at Victoria's Platform 1 with the up 'Night Ferry' on 2 May 1967, conveying Wagon Lits sleeping cars from Paris and Brussels via the Calais – Dover train ferry. The leading three vehicles are luggage vans or 'fourgons' to S.N.C.F. design but British loading gauge. ***Brian Stephenson***

Telephones
TICKETS AND ENQUIRIES
CONTINENT
CHANNEL ISLANDS
75
THE NIGHT FERRY
PARIS BRUSSELS

HALL & Cº

Opposite: The Bulleid/Raworth 'booster' electric locomotives 20001-20003 were first tried out on the Newhaven boat train in 1949 and from then until their withdrawal were regular performers on this demanding duty, although their use diminished from 1964. In early 1960s condition with lined bright green livery and folding headcode discs, 20003 approaches Clapham Junction with the early morning up working to Victoria in about 1961, overtaking a 4-EPB unit on a mundane suburban service. ***Brian Stephenson***

Six years earlier sister locomotive 20001 passes Cooksbridge with an up Newhaven boat train on 14 August 1955. The black livery adopted for these locomotives in 1950 is by now looking rather tired, and the coaches all carry crimson and cream livery, soon to be superseded by green. The train includes an eclectic mix of stock, some of it by now quite elderly, including Maunsell boat train coaches and 'non-descript' saloons. ***R. C. Riley/The Transport Treasury***

4-CEP 7127 leads this CEP+BEP+CEP formation down Grosvenor Bank into Victoria on 19 May 1963 with the 16.42 boat train arrival from Folkestone Harbour via Ashford and Maidstone East, conveying cross-channel ferry passengers from Calais. Battersea power station dominates the skyline of this view, taken from a passing 4-SUB on a Central Section suburban service. ***Brian Stephenson***

An unidentified type HA E5000 locomotive departs from Victoria (Eastern) and crosses over to the Central Section lines with the 09.31 down Newhaven Harbour boat train on 5 June 1966. The eleven-coach set is formed with a mixture of Bulleid and B.R. vehicles, all in green. Close observation shows that the locomotive is lacking its pantograph. On the right a sister locomotive has just arrived with the inbound 'Night Ferry' and is heading light to Stewarts Lane. ***Brian Stephenson***

Brand new type JB electro-diesel E6029 uncouples from the 08.22 special boat train from Victoria organised by L.C.G.B. and the Railway Magazine at Folkestone Harbour on 15 May 1966. This was the very first revenue-earning duty for this locomotive. After crossing the English Channel to Calais, travellers would either participate in 'The Somme Rail Tour' or The Picardy Rail Tour'. ***Brian Stephenson***

On 22 May 1968, type HB electro-diesel E6104 makes use of its 650hp Paxman diesel engine to haul the empty stock of a Waterloo - Southampton Ocean Liner Terminal boat train back over the eastern dock lines to Northam Junction, where it will regain the third rail. The train is formed almost entirely of Mark1 compartment firsts. The ten members of this class were converted at Crewe from type HA straight electric locomotives for the Bournemouth electrification, but proved unsuccessful and had a working life of barely ten years. ***John H. Bird/www.anistr.com***

Motor Luggage Van (MLV) 68003 stands Dover Priory carriage sidings in about 1963, still in original condition with whistles and plain green ends. Designed mainly for use on Kent Coast boat trains, these vehicles were basically motorised full brakes with a suburban-style full-width cab at each end, giving added security for conveying bonded luggage and freight. They were also dual-braked and had batteries enabling them to work short distances over unelectrified quayside lines, even hauling a limited trailing load. ***Chris Wilson Collection***

The evening down 'Night Ferry', with type HA E5011 in charge, passes Beckenham Junction in 1968, conveying Wagon Lits sleeping cars to Paris and Brussels via the Dover – Calais train ferry. The train comprises three Mark 1 vehicles including a restaurant car, five sleeping cars and three baggage vans. Although of typical Wagon Lits design and carrying the distinctive blue livery, the cars were designed for the British loading gauge and were therefore somewhat more cramped than their Continental cousins. ***Chris Wilson Collection***

The three Co-Co electric locomotives quickly and inevitably became known as 'Hornby's after the well-known make of toy electric trains. 20001 in black livery oversees a second up Newhaven boat train near Cooksbridge on 14 August 1955. Another very varied selection of coaches, including a number still in Southern green, suggests this was a relief working. ***R. C. Riley / The Transport Treasury***

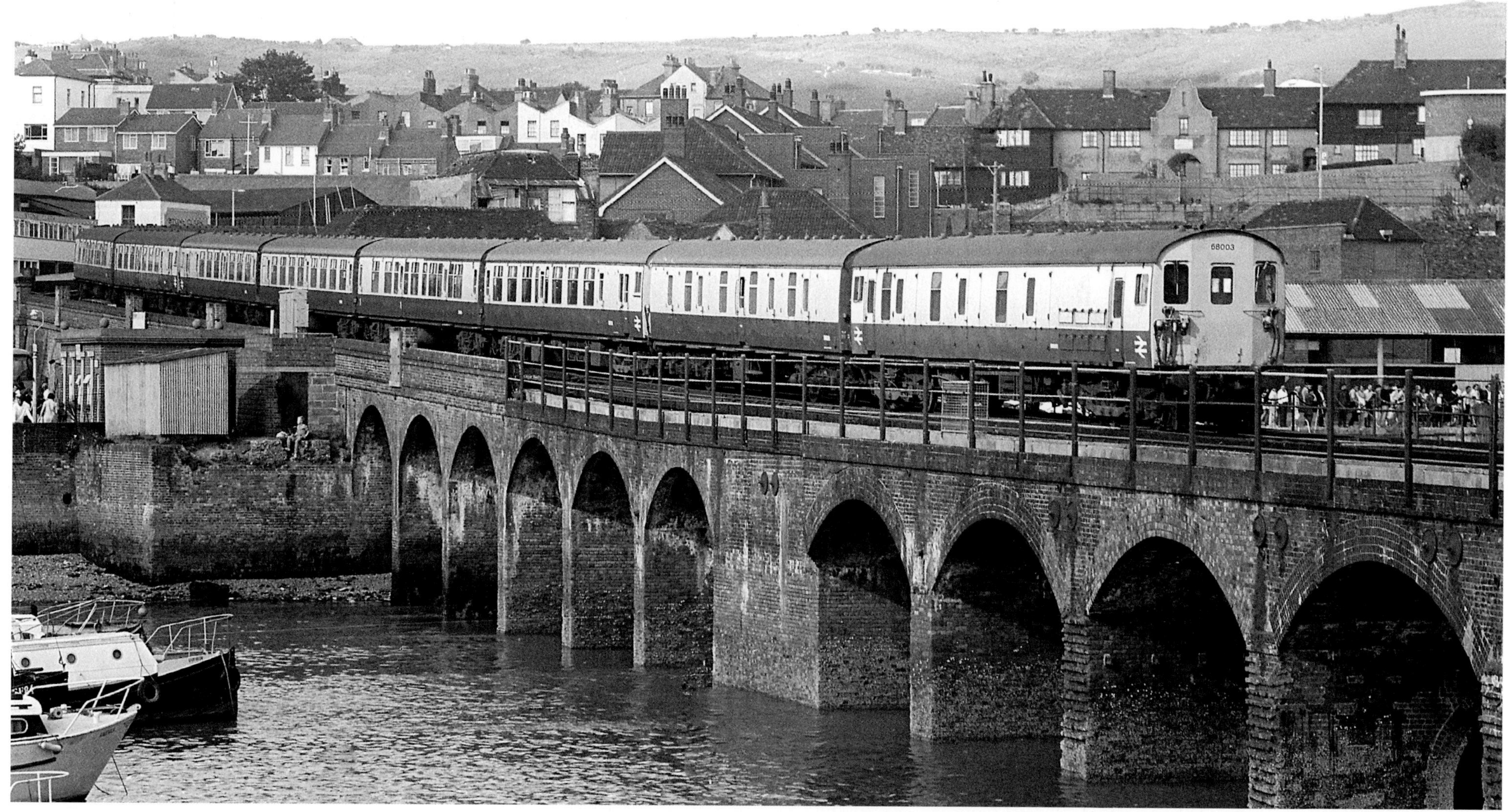

MLV 68003 leads a trailer luggage van (TLV) and a CEP+BEP+CEP formation approaching Folkestone Harbour with a boat train from Victoria in July 1970. By this time virtually all Kent Coast express stock was in blue/grey livery. The TLVs were converted in 1967 from Mark 1 BG full brakes to provide extra space for bonded baggage on boat trains, as use of two MLVs strained the power supply somewhat. Modifications included installing the necessary through wiring and jumper cables for multiple unit operation and sealing of the end gangways. They had only a short life due to Trade Union difficulties regarding their manning. ***Rail Photoprints***

BOAC BOAC
BOAC
42
E6012
GOLDEN ARROW

Opposite: One of the first type JB electro-diesels, E6012, hauls the 11.00 'Golden Arrow' boat train to Folkestone Harbour out of Victoria on 13 November 1966. The new British Rail double arrow symbol has recently been added to the bodysides. With only 1600hp available as compared to the 2550hp of the HA 'booster' locomotives, E6012 would have struggled getting this heavy train up Grosvenor Bank.
Brian Stephenson

Right: The boat train platform at Newhaven Harbour was located on a short spur just south of the platforms on the Seaford branch, and gave continental passengers direct access to the quayside. Shortly after arrival, Co-Co 'booster' locomotive 20002 has detached from the stock of the boat train from Victoria on an unrecorded date in 1960.
Chris Wilson Collection

In gleaming lined green livery and resplendent with a new headboard, flags and side arrows, type HA electric locomotive E5015 departs from Victoria Platform 8 in charge of the 11.00 'Golden Arrow' Pullman boat train to Dover Marine on 9 July 1961. This flagship service had first been electrically hauled the previous month on 18 June, and for some time E5015 was maintained in immaculate external condition to haul it. Even the two green Bulleid coaches seem particularly well-polished. ***Brian Stephenson***

Type HA E5006 approaches Catford with the up 'Night Ferry' on the morning of 8 August 1959. With only phase 1 of the Kent Coast electrification completed, it would have been routed via Faversham. As with the 'Golden Arrow', a new headboard has been provided to suit the electric locomotives. ***David Brown Collection***

Left: Type JB electro-diesel E6029 passes New Wandsworth in dappled light with the up early morning Newhaven boat train in late summer 1969. The train is by now composed entirely of electrically heated B.R. Mark 1 stock in blue and grey livery. *Brian Stephenson*

Opposite: Isle of Wight 4-VEC unit 043 stands at Ryde Pier Head waiting to depart with the pier shuttle to Ryde Esplanade, which connected with the foot-passenger ferry from Portsmouth Harbour, in July 1970. The IoW electric stock was refurbished from former London Transport 'standard' tube stock cars dating from 1923-31 and entered service between Ryde and Shanklin in March 1967. The pier shuttle replaced the petrol trams which ran on separate tracks along the pier until January 1969.
Gordon Edgar/Rail Photoprints

2
D
043

46
GOLDEN ARROW
BOAC

Opposite: Type HA E5007 climbs out of Victoria with the 11.00 'Golden Arrow' in September 1966. Now in plain green livery without lining, it carries the headboard, but no flags nor arrows and the general impression is by now not quite so sparkling. The vehicle behind the locomotive is an S.R. four-wheeled and wooden-bodied utility van. *Chris Wilson Collection*

Right: It was the turn of almost-new type JB electro-diesel E6013 to haul the down 'Golden Arrow' on Sunday 13 November 1966. Complete with headboard and rather grubby flags, it waits to depart from platform 7 at Victoria. Headcode '42' indicates that the train will on this occasion be diverted to Folkestone Harbour and run via Swanley, Maidstone East and Ashford.
Chris Wilson Collection

4-RES unit 3072, temporarily without its 'cafeteria car' but with 6-PUL Pullman composite 'Brenda' marshalled between the first class compartments and the rear motor coach, passes Earlswood with a Redhill – Lover's Walk (Brighton) test train on 2 November 1956. These tests were in connection with replacing the existing poorly-riding 'Dutch' equalising bar bogies of the 6-PUL and 5-BEL stock. It is likely that the C.M.E.E. staff on board were treated to Pullman refreshments at some point on the trip. Note the reversed headcode stencil. ***J. J. Smith/Bluebell Museum Archive***

Opposite: The 14.00 down 'Brighton Belle', formed with ten cars led by 5-BEL 3053, is nicely framed by an overbridge south of Hassocks on an unknown date in the summer of 1971. Romantic though the 'Belle' was, by this time it was hopelessly uneconomic to operate, and the 1932 constructed units were considered life-expired, even though they sat most of the Second World War out in store. In the eyes of some the superior Pullman service levels put British Rail's catering efforts to shame.
Chris Wilson Collection

3053
4
BRIGHTON BELLE
BRIGHTON BELLE

Type JB electro-diesel E6022 has just run around the empties of the 'Bournemouth Belle' Pullman at Branksome, after they have been serviced at the new Bournemouth electric depot sited on the closed Bournemouth West station approach. It will now take the train to Bournemouth to pick up passengers for the afternoon 16.45 return to Waterloo. The 'Bournemouth Belle' was a casualty of the Bournemouth electrification scheme, last running on Sunday 9 July 1967, and this view was taken on the previous day. ***John H. Bird/www.anistr.com***

6-PUL 3007 runs into East Croydon with a Victoria – Littlehampton via Hove express in 1965. Twenty of these 6-PUL units were built in 1932 for express services to Brighton and Worthing, but by 1938 they also worked to Eastbourne, Ore and Littlehampton as successive coastal electrification schemes were completed. Each unit included a Pullman Composite Car of exactly the same style as those in the 5-BELs, from which staff served light refreshments both to supplement-paying passengers in the car itself and in adjacent vehicles. ***Chris Wilson Collection***

5-BEL 3053 on the short-lived 17.45 Eastbourne to Victoria 'Eastbourne Belle' passes Chetington, near Cooksbridge on the line between Lewes and Keymer Junction, on 27 August 1950. This service, which ran on summer Sundays only, was inaugurated on 6 June 1948 in a bout of post-war optimism but was never particularly popular and only lasted until 15 September 1957. ***J. J. Smith/Bluebell Museum Archive***

5-BEL 3053 is once again seen this speeding through the 1958 Gatwick Airport station with the 15.00 down 'Brighton Belle' in about 1960. Rebuilt from the closed racecourse station in connection with redevelopment of the airport slightly to the north of the previous site, the original signal box was retained among the new footbridge, canopies and lighting. A typical mercury-arc rectifier substation of the type provided for the 1932-33 electrification is visible to the right. ***R. K. Blencowe Collection***

6-PUL 3008 has clearly just returned to service after a repaint as it passes Clapham Junction with the 14.00 Victoria – Brighton non-stop service in the summer of 1964, and Pullman Composite Car 'Lorna' is almost glowing. Yellow warning panels were not common on the Brighton express stock and most were withdrawn without receiving them, 3008 survived until March 1966. ***Brian Stephenson***

3013
52

Opposite: Seen from the A3 Battersea Rise bridge, 6-PUL 3013, including Pullman Car 'Brenda', has just passed Clapham Junction with the 11.45 Victoria – Eastbourne – Ore service on 28 March 1965. Although in the same livery as 3008 on the previous page it is somewhat less sparkling, but it ran in service for a further year. ***Brian Stephenson***

Only two 5-BEL units were required to operate the 'Brighton Belle' service and the spare unit was available for specials or private hire when not undergoing maintenance. It was even used by Royalty on occasion. On Wednesday 19 April 1961, 3051 was used for a private charter from Blackfriars to Eastbourne and is seen here soon after departing from London at 12.35pm. The train was hired by Unilever to take London-based staff to the company's Annual Conference in Eastbourne.
J. J. Smith/Bluebell Museum Archive

Here is a second view of Stewarts Lane's dedicated 'Golden Arrow' locomotive E5015 awaiting departure from Victoria's platform 7 with the 11.00 down working, again in pristine condition and displaying headboard, flags and arrows. On this occasion, again soon after the start of electric haulage, there were no ordinary coaches at the front of the train, the leading Pullman car being coupled directly behind the utility van. *C. R. L. Coles/Rail Archive Stephenson*

Above: Having recently been outshopped in blue and grey but still retaining its stencil headcode panel, 5-BEL 3052 approaches Clapham Junction with the 14.00 down 'Brighton Belle' on 6 February 1969. ***John Scrace***

A regular duty for the 'Hornby' Co-Co's in their later years was the Royal specials from Victoria to Tattenham Corner on Derby Day. As always specially prepared for the occasion by Stewarts Lane staff, 20002 is in charge on Wednesday 2 June 1965, and is seen here negotiating Gloucester Road flyover between Selhurst and East Croydon. The train includes a Royal Saloon and three Pullman cars. ***J.J. Smith/Bluebell Museum Archive***

Left: Another excellent vantage point from which to view and photograph trains on the Brighton main line was the bridge just north of Earlswood station, where the Redhill and Quarry lines came back together. 5-BEL 3052 passes at speed with the 11.00 down 'Brighton Belle' on 10 August 1958. ***Chris Wilson Collection***

Opposite: 5-BEL 3051 waits to depart with another non-stop 'Brighton Belle' service to Victoria on 23 August 1963. This fine portrait of the cab end shows in detail the larger Pullman crest adopted in 1960 and applied to units 3051 and 3052. The electric Pullmans were of all-steel construction and efforts were made in their design to keep all panelling as flush as possible.
John H. Bird/www.anistr.com

3051
4

3019
4

Opposite: 6-PUL 3019, leading the 10.00 Victoria – Brighton non-stop, passes Wandsworth Common on 26 May 1963. It has just gained first class cantrail strips. By having a composite trailer on either side, there was access to first class compartments from both halves of the unit when Pullman Car 'Peggy' was locked out of use. ***Brian Stephenson***

This undated view from about 1971 during their last summer of operation shows 5-BEL 3052 as the leading unit in this formation passing Tooting Bec Common between Balham and Streatham Common with the 14.00 down 'Brighton Belle'. ***Chris Wilson Collection***

6-PUL 3010 leads a 6-PAN with an Ore – Eastbourne – Victoria service passing Ditchling Common, between Plumpton and Keymer Junction, on Sunday 13 June 1965. The signal box in the background controls Spatham Lane level crossing and slightly closer is one of the Southern's characteristic track-paralleling huts, located between pairs of substations to minimize voltage-drop within sections on the third-rail circuits.
Patrick Russell/Rail Archive Stephenson

Pullman Composite 'Naomi', formed within 6-PUL unit 3011, poses at East Croydon in about 1965. From left to right, the internal arrangements comprised a very compact kitchen and pantry, a two-bay first class saloon with eight armchairs, a first class coupe compartment with four armchairs, a lavatory, and finally a second class saloon with sixteen seats arranged two+two either side of a centre gangway. These cars were generally similar in every respect to the 5-BELs and rode equally badly. Photographs of the single Pullman cars are surprisingly rare. ***Chris Wilson Collection***

5-BEL 3053 runs into Brighton from Lover's Walk, where she would have been serviced and re-supplied before working the late lunchtime 13.25 'Brighton Belle' service to Victoria in around 1964. 3053 kept her old-style, smaller, Pullman crests until repainting in 1969. *Chris Wilson Collection*

Opposite: 20003 departs from Victoria with Pullman race special in June 1963, probably bound for Epsom Downs during Derby Week. The Pullman staff will no doubt see to it that the punters on board will already be 'well oiled' when they arrive. ***Brian Stephenson***

BISHOP & SONS
REMOVALS &
PULLMAN
VE.144

3053
P

Opposite: 5-BEL unit 3053 is nicely illuminated as she stands at Victoria after arrival with the 13.25 'Brighton Belle' from the coast on 24 March 1955. The headcode has not yet been attached for the 15.00 down working.
C. R. L. Coles/Rail Archive Stephenson

Right: 6-PUL 3010, incorporating Pullman Car 'Daisy', calls at St Leonards Warrior Square with an Ore – Victoria express on 13 June 1965. On arrival at Eastbourne it will attach to a 6-PAN already in the platform to form a twelve-car train for the run to London.
Patrick Russell/Rail Archive Stephenson

Take Care at Crossings

This atmospheric view shows 2-BIL 2037 descending from the Arun bridge and about to pass over the level crossing as it approaches Ford leading a pair of sister units on a Brighton – Portsmouth working in early 1970. Prominent are the guard's periscopes fitted to the roofs of virtually all new S.R. electric stock from 1932. Unit 2037 retained its rather faded green livery until withdrawal in April 1970, but then had a short reprieve in departmental use as an 'air brake test unit' at Derby Research Centre. Opposite: At the same location but from the opposite side of the line, blue-liveried 2-HAL 2645 leads a Victoria – Gatwick Airport – Bognor Regis stopping service. This unit came out of passenger service in December 1970 and was then converted into 2-PAN 064, specifically to carry parcels in the pre-Christmas period. It was used again for this purpose in 1971 and was broken up the following year. ***Both: John H. Bird/www.anistr.com***

WAY OUT
TICKET OFFICE
& ENQUIRIES
4
6
FORD
2645
98
DANGER
DON'T TOUCH
CONDUCTOR RAILS
NO EXIT
THROUGH SUBWAY
FOR DOWN TRAINS
PASSENGERS
MUST NOT CROSS
THE LINE HERE
NO EXIT
WAY OUT
THROUGH
SUBWAY
PASSENGERS
MUST NOT CROSS
THE LINE HERE

6046
94

Opposite: 2-HAP 6046 crosses the Great Stour river and a small gated crossing as it departs from Chartham with a Canterbury West to Victoria stopping service via Ashford and Maidstone East on 3 March 1968.
Brian Stephenson

A pair of 2-BIL units led by 2094 passes the Southdown bus garage and crosses Basin Road on the approach to Chichester with a Brighton – Portsmouth Harbour service on 24 March 1969.
John H. Bird/www.anistr.com

BEDHAMPTON HALT
Seaspeed
to Europe
from
Dover
–fast and fun!
TO THE ISLE OF WIGHT
Seaspeed
7716
73
PRIVATE

Opposite: One of the twenty original 4-VEP units built for the Bournemouth electrification, 7716, pulls out of Bedhampton Halt with Portsmouth & Southsea – Waterloo stopping service on 5 May 1969. Notable features include the cast aluminium 'double arrow', blue-painted window frames and the short-lived yellow destination board slotted in above the cab side window. The notice board at the bottom of the footbridge is still headed by a 'Southern Electric' logo dating from the 1937 electrification. ***John H. Bird/www.anistr.com***

Minor maintenance work is taking place at Newhaven Town level crossing as blue 2-HAL 2629 leads an unidentified green 2-BIL into the station with a Brighton – Seaford service in the spring of 1971. 2629 was one of the last survivors and was in traffic on the final day of operation, 29 July 1971. The traditional gates have given way to an interesting staggered raised barrier set up to suit the wider than usual road location here. ***John Day/Rail Photoprints***

4-CIG unit 7332, in original green with small warning panel, pulls out of Havant and crosses New Lane level crossing with a morning Portsmouth Harbour – Victoria via Horsham and Sutton service on 7 January 1970. Four or eight coaches from Bognor Regis, including a 4 BEP buffet unit, will be attached at Barnham. Unit 7332 was one of the last 4-CIGs to retain green livery, being repainted blue and grey in June 1970. Havant station was reconstructed in 1937 in the 'moderne' style with the usual extensive use of concrete and steel as favoured by the Southern. ***John H. Bird/www.anistr.com***

Passengers off the train wait to cross the line as 2-BIL 2019 starts away from Ford with a Portsmouth – Brighton stopping service in 1967. In the down loop fellow 2-BIL unit number 2004, one of the earlier 1934 build identifiable by the ventilator bonnets above the door droplights, waits to depart for Littlehampton. Both units would remain in their green livery with yellow warning panels until withdrawal. Unit 2004 went first in March 1969 and was scrapped by Armytage Ltd of Sheepbridge, whereas 2019 hung on a little longer until January 1970 and was sent to Cashmore's of Newport for its disposal. ***John Vaughan/Chris Wilson Collection***

Not long in service, type JB electro-diesel E6043 is working on diesel power as it hauls a brake van and former 6-PAN motor coach from withdrawn unit 3031 on Bournemouth line conductor-rail gauging trials near Millbrook on 6 January 1967. The PAN vehicle was particularly suitable for these tests as it had pick-up shoes on both bogies, as would the new 4-REP units. Opposite: An earlier built Type JA electro-diesel E6003 propels a rake of three new 4-CIG units into Fareham in November 1965 during early push-pull trials in preparation for the Bournemouth electrification, where such a system would be used on a regular basis. Running over a non-electrified line, the 27-wire control system enabled the 600hp diesel of the locomotive to be controlled from the driving cab of the leading electric unit. Performance with twelve vehicles would not have been sparkling, however. ***Both: John H. Bird/www.anistr.com***

Not in Passenger Service

Another two of the six pre-production 1600hp electro-diesels of type JA, E6004 and E6001, pass Bickley Junction heading eastwards with a test rake of green Mark 1 coaches on 28 September 1964. The JAs were designed in the Brighton Works drawing office, and their domed roofline above the cabs has clearly been copied from the 5-BEL units which passed several times each day. ***Chris Wilson Collection***

Opposite: Kent Coast type HA 'booster' locomotives E5016 and E5000 pass Copyhold Junction with an interesting northbound test train, comprising three Bulleid coaches and nine loaded coal hoppers, on Sunday 23 October 1960. Copyhold Junction was where the electrified branch to Ardingly and Horsted Keynes, closed to passengers in September 1963, diverged from the main Brighton line north of Haywards Heath.
J. J. Smith/Bluebell Museum Archive

8

Stripped of their original London Transport livery and markings, four 'Standard' tube stock cars making up a 4-VEC unit for the forthcoming Isle of Wight electrification reverse in platform 4 at Wimbledon on 9 July 1966. They are en-route from L.T. Acton Works, where electrical overhaul and conversion to third rail took place, to Stewarts Lane for painting in B.R. blue with full yellow ends. To the left a 4-SUB unit pulls into platform 5 with a Waterloo bound suburban service, while in platform 2 a train of District Line R Stock is about to head off to Earl's Court and beyond.
J. J. Smith/Bluebell Museum Archive

A prototype Motor Luggage Van (MLV), numbered NE 68000, was built at Eastleigh for the Newcastle – South Shields line. Before being sent to Tyneside it was trialled on the S.R. and is seen here on Monday 5 December 1955 passing Earlswood with the 12.45 Norwood Junction – Horsham Goods test train, hauling a quite substantial load of goods wagons. With de-electrification in 1963 on Tyneside it was transferred to the Liverpool – Southport line and was withdrawn in 1967. ***J. J. Smith/Bluebell Museum Archive***

A pair of de-icing units led by 97, converted from withdrawn suburban motor coaches in 1960, are parked in a siding adjacent to the coal loading incline at Durnsford Road power station on 19 March 1961, three years after it stopped supplying traction current to South Western suburban lines. Wholesale renewal of lineside cabling is clearly taking place, as evidenced by the large stacks of concrete cable troughing. 2-HAL and 4-RES units are just visible in sidings behind the concrete supports. The site was eventually cleared during the first months of 1965. *Dr Terry Gough/The Transport Library*

An earlier view from the other side of the ramp, dated 9 February 1957, shows the unique Dick-Kerr Bo-Bo locomotive 74s which was employed shunting loaded coal wagons up the incline to the hoppers above the coal storage shed at the top. 74s was originally built for shunting purposes on the Waterloo and City tube in 1899 but was transferred to Durnsford Road in 1914 and remained there until the power station was shut down. Livery is unconfirmed, but it was generally grubby with coal dust anyway. ***R. C. Riley/The Transport Treasury***

95

Opposite: Self-propelled de-icing unit 95 is parked at Knights Hill sidings, Tulse Hill, on 10 September 1960 when first converted. These units were modified at Stewarts Lane and Peckham Rye from 1925-vintage 'long-frame' motor coaches of withdrawn 4-SUB units in the '4326' series. They replaced similar units and unpowered vans which had L.B.S.C.R. wooden bodywork, as seen on page 96 (bottom).
R. C. Riley/The Transport Treasury

New Kent Coast trailer de-icing van DS 70087 and de-icing unit 101 and are parked outside Peckham Rye depot on Boxing Day 1960. Oddly, the unit is S.R. green but the van carries service stock red/brown livery. The vehicles were fitted with tanks containing de-icing fluid, piped onto the conductor rails through tubes attached to shoe-beams on the trailer bogies. As they were out for long periods on cold winter nights, they also contained toilets and mess facilities. ***R. C. Riley/The Transport Treasury***

Kent Coast de-icing van DS 70051, converted from all-steel augmentation trailer 10399 formerly formed in 4-SUB 4351, stands at Ramsgate, out of use for the summer, in about 1964. These vans were equipped with electro-pneumatic braking and buckeye couplers specifically for routes in Kent, as they could then work coupled to EPB, HAP and CEP stock which other de-icing units could not. ***Chris Wilson Collection***

Trailer de-icing van DS 398 was converted from trailer set vehicle 9079 and is seen parked at Wimbledon Park on 21 April 1956. Problems with iced-up conductor rails during the winter led the S.R. in 1947 to convert a number of withdrawn trailer set vehicles of L.B.S.C.R. origin into these de-icing vans, which spread a specially-formulated warm oil onto the conductor rail surface intended to melt ice which had already formed and discourage more from freezing. Operating to set diagrams from the various EMU depots when freezing conditions were forecast, they ran between electric units or were even sometimes hauled by steam engines. Behind is one of the post-war all-steel HAL-type trailer composites of a 'hybrid' 2-BIL unit. ***J. H. Aston***

A second view at Peckham Rye on 26 December 1960 shows all of green de-icing unit 101 and the rusty red coloured de-icing vans DS 70087 and DS 70086, the last of their respective types to be converted. The positions of the toilet facilities are obvious from this angle.
R. C. Riley/The Transport Treasury

017

Opposite: Although still green, by 1969 de-icing unit 017 (now renumbered from 98) had gained wrap-around yellow ends and roller-blind headcode panels and is seen stored for the summer at Fratton depot. The downward-facing periscopes enabled the operator to control the flow of de-icing fluid depending on the conductor rail position, whilst remaining safely inside within the warmth of the coach shielded from the harsh weather conditions prevailing. ***Chris Wilson Collection***

De-icing unit 002 is parked at Bournemouth depot in about 1969. Three of these units were converted from HAL-type motor brake seconds in 1968-69 for the Bournemouth line. In fact, five of the six vehicles concerned came from 4-LAV units 2926 and 2954-55, which had this style of motor coach. The reconstruction included re-equipping with modern controls and electro-pneumatic brakes, and the frontal appearance was considerably changed by the fitting of almost-flush roller blind headcodes. ***John H. Bird/www.anistr.com***

This departmental test unit numbered as 051 was formed from surplus former L.M.R. London area D.C. electric stock and was used for trials of new bogie designs in connection with the PEP prototype sliding-door units. With motor coach DS 975029 leading, it passes Swaythling at speed on a run down the Bournemouth main line on an unrecorded date in April 1970. These units were originally built at Eastleigh in 1957-58 and the family resemblance to contemporary S.R. EPB and HAP stock is obvious. ***Colour Rail***

Departmental C.M.E.E. stores unit 023 passes through platform 3 at Gatwick Airport with the 12.06 stores working from Selhurst to Lover's Walk depot on a Saturday in 1970. 023 was converted from a pair of HAL motor coaches that year to convey parts between depots and, with sister unit 022, worked to regular weekly schedules. 4-VEP 7803 in platform 2 is waiting with its gangway door open for a coastal service to arrive and to couple together for the journey to Victoria, and its yellow end throws a strange reflection on the side of 023. ***Chris Wilson Collection***

7803
7803
023
04
DS70316

HALL & Co
16

Opposite: Bulleid Co-Co 'booster' locomotive 20003, in final condition with roller-blind headcode and small warning panel, heads a short van train comprising one S.R. utility van and two GUVs approaching Clapham Junction northbound in March 1968. Headcode '16' suggests that the vans come from Littlehampton, Worthing or Hove. 20003 was outshopped in this livery to haul the Royal Train from Victoria to Tattenham Corner for the June 1967 Derby, and retained it until withdrawal in September 1968.
Brian Stephenson

Right: The Southern's seldom-seen Instruction Unit S10 stands at Ramsgate depot in 1960. This interesting departmental unit was converted in 1956 from the pre-war coaches of 4-SUB 4579, which had L.S.W.R. bodywork, into a mobile classroom which could visit depots for staff training where facilities would not otherwise exist. The three vehicles contained a lecture room and demonstration examples of brake, control, heating, lighting and signalling equipment. S10 was generally parked in inaccessible sidings and rarely moved, so was difficult to photograph.
Strathwood Library Collection

3042
16
8
8

Opposite: Unit 3042 heads a pair of 6-CORs, from a class of ten made up using redundant 6-PUL and 6-PAN stock in 1965-66 as spares, passing Bromley South in March 1967 with a Ramsgate – Stewarts Lane driver training run. This was in preparation for their use on Victoria – Ramsgate peak services and summer extras, for which they were used sporadically for two summers. Unsurprisingly, given their age and rough riding, they were unpopular both with crews and passengers alike. Their final duties were on peak-hour London Bridge – Hove trains in early November 1968. ***Brian Stephenson***

Above: There is no doubt that all the signalmen in the area and the motormen working their services alike would have to be even more alert than usual when permanent way occupations were taking place, perhaps even more so at busy locations such as this. Type JB electro-diesel E6042 is in charge of a short engineer's train on the down Central suburban line at Clapham Junction in September 1968, as track maintenance work, involving replacement of conductor rail insulators, is being carried out on the up line. ***Brian Stephenson***

Co-Co 'booster' locomotive 20003 is still in in black livery as it passes through platform 4 at East Croydon with a northbound freight, probably bound for Norwood Yard, on 9 July 1955. Although there are many images of this class on passenger workings in this book, their main use was on heavy fitted goods trains between the main Central Section yards such as Norwood, Three Bridges, Chichester and Polegate. ***J. F. Davies/Rail Archive Stephenson***

This slightly earlier view shows sister locomotive 20001 departing from the electrified reception road in Chichester Yard with the 09.56 MX mixed freight bound for Norwood Yard on 12 April 1952. At this time, Chichester was the interchange point for goods traffic between the S.R. Central and Western Sections. It was common to see a 'Hornby' parked between duties at the buffer stops in the down bay at Chichester station, strange electrical clicking emanating from is internals to intrigue schoolboys. ***C. R. L. Coles/Rail Archive Stephenson***

Type HA E5014 oversees a freight train at Faversham in February 1965. It is utilising its pantograph to collect current from the overhead trolley wires installed in some freight yards during the Kent Coast electrification where it was considered too hazardous to lay conductor rails. E5014 is in overall plain dark green livery, its B.R. badge almost obscured by grime. ***Chris Wilson Collection***

Opposite: New type JB electro-diesel E6027 passes Brentford Central on the Hounslow loop with an eastbound freight comprising fitted vans on 10 September 1966. This route was an important freight artery connecting Feltham yard with the northern main lines via Kew East Junction. A parcels van is parked in the dock behind the train and some interesting period road coaches occupy the yard. ***Brian Stephenson***

HONEYWELL
7H
Richards

6K
E6003

Opposite: The third type JA electro-diesel, E6003, makes use of its slow-speed control on 600hp diesel power while passing through the unloading facility with a 'merry-go-round' coal train at the C.E.G.B. Richborough generating station on 18 March 1964. This official view clearly shows another livery variation tried on these locomotives; the lower bodysides are light grey and the yellow warning panel has been omitted.
David Brown Collection

Class 74 HB electro-diesel E6103, probably just released for traffic after overhaul given its shiny front and white pipework, passes Christchurch with up van train bound for Clapham Yard on 28 November 1972. These locomotives had a solid-state control system which gave much trouble throughout their lives. An S.R. engineer was quoted as saying that what these unfortunate locomotives taught him was: "Never convert anything".
Chris Wilson Collection

Everyday Service

Opposite: At about midday on Saturday 18 June 1955, 2-BIL unit 2071 is picked out by the strong sunlight at Waterloo and will shortly be departing with a stopping service to Portsmouth and Southsea. Headcode 57 indicates there is no Alton portion on this train, being instead run separately to allow for the expected holiday crowds on the Portsmouth service. Keen-eyed aficionados will note 4-COR 3158 in the background, with unique trailer composite 11861 which had been converted after the war from spare 4-RES trailer dining first 11132 by reconfiguring the dining area into a sixteen-seat third class saloon arranged 3+1 with an off-centre gangway.
Alan A. Jackson/Chris Wilson Collection

Above: The motorman chats to a porter as 2-SL unit 1806 calls at South Bermondsey with a London Bridge – Victoria South London line service on 21 August 1954. The end of the canopy shows evidence of repairs following wartime bomb damage, inevitably commonplace throughout this part of south London, after so many after dark attacks by the Luftwaffe during the blitz and later on from the 'doodlebugs'. The wooden island platform was provided when the station was re-sited in 1929 following track rearrangements; previously it had been on the London side of the junction with the main line.
Alan A. Jackson/Chris Wilson Collection

4119
36

Opposite: 4-SUB 4119, from the first batch of ten new units with all-steel bodywork turned out from Eastleigh Works in 1946, departs from Crystal Palace with the 10.26 Victoria – Beckenham Junction service on 31 August 1965. Although accommodation was all in 'six-a-side' compartments, they had slightly more legroom than the preceding 'Sheba' units 4101-10. ***Brian Stephenson***

Right: 4-SUB 4307 is dwarfed by the gaunt skeleton of Cannon Street's overall roof as it departs with an evening peak service to Dartford via Greenwich on Friday 16 September 1955. 4307 was built as 'short-frame' three-car suburban unit 1292 for the 1925 Guildford and Dorking electrification, augmented to a 4-SUB with a new 'six-a-side' trailer in October 1945 and withdrawn in April 1960. The roof framework at Cannon Street was dismantled in 1958.
R.C. Riley/The Transport Treasury

2-NOL 1849 stands in the electrified platform at Horsted Keynes, waiting to depart with the hourly stopping service to Haywards Heath and Seaford on 15 March 1958. The two young gentlemen smartly attired on the left appear to be railway enthusiast 'escapees' from nearby Ardingly College, served by the next station on the branch. ***Chris Wilson Collection***

2-HAP units 6102 and 6087 are about to depart from Lymington Pier for Brockenhurst on 2 June 1967, the first day of electric working on the branch. Being on the quayside, this station was largely of wooden construction to keep it lightweight, and its arc-sectioned canopy still gave it a vintage L.S.W.R. air. From here, passengers and cars could cross the Solent by ferry to Yarmouth on the Isle of Wight. *John H. Bird/www.anistr.com*

2-HAL 2648, in green with full yellow ends, stands in the bay platform at Seaford waiting to return to Lewes and Brighton on 4 January 1969. The black digits of the unit number are not very level. 2648 was withdrawn at the end of January 1971, still in green, and was scrapped the following July. ***Chris Wilson Collection***

An original former L.S.W.R. 'nutcracker' 4-SUB unit 4149, dating from 1916 but later rebuilt onto new underframes and then augmented to four coaches with an additional L.S.W.R.-bodied vehicle from a disbanded trailer set, calls at Motspur Park working an Effingham Junction – Waterloo service on 2 October 1955. 4149 was withdrawn the following month but its underframes and bogies, suitably refurbished, were incorporated into new 4-EPB vehicles. The inter-war suburban housing developments as seen here were strongly encouraged by railway electrification and the construction of new stations, Motspur Park itself being opened on a green-field site in 1925. ***Dr Terry Gough/The Transport Library***

Signs of wartime damage and patching-up are still very evident in this view of Charing Cross, when photographed on 9 May 1953. On the left an eight-car formation of 2-HAL units, with 2687 leading, prepares to depart with a service to Gillingham via Greenwich, Dartford, Gravesend and Strood, where a portion will be detached for Maidstone West. On the right augmented 4-SUB 4579, with L.S.W.R. bodywork, has just arrived with an inbound service. ***Alan A. Jackson/Chris Wilson Collection***

2-HAL 2618 leads a rake of four units passing Shortlands with the 12.18 Victoria – Maidstone East and Gillingham service, dividing at Swanley, on 1 September 1954. The second unit is one of the post-war 'all steel' examples from the 2693-99 series, built to make-good war losses. Images of 2-HAL units working on the Maidstone and Gillingham lines in the 1948-58 period are surprisingly uncommon. ***John Head/Rail Archive Stephenson***

4-LAV unit 2922 calls at the original 1935 Gatwick Airport station with a Brighton – Victoria via Redhill semi-fast service in the spring of 1958, just before closure on 27 May. It was replaced by the modernised racecourse station a little to the north, also called Gatwick Airport. The 1935 concrete footbridge would, however, live on, as it was removed to Balcombe when platforms there were extended to take twelve cars as part of the Gatwick scheme. ***Chris Wilson Collection***

The two experimental 4-DD units, 4002 and 4001, pause at Waterloo East with an empty working ready to form the 18.04 Charing Cross-Dartford via Sidcup service on 12 May 1969. Problems with low route availability, slow loading and unloading, unreliable ventilation fans and public safety issues ensured that this interesting but flawed design was not perpetuated. The pair nonetheless remained in service until October 1971, latterly operating only at the shoulders of the morning and evening peaks.
John H. Bird/www.anistr.com

The prototype 'Sheba' 4-SUB 4101, unveiled in 1941, approaches Brentford Central with an anti-clockwise Hounslow loop service on 10 September 1966. By this time, it was painted in the second SR green livery with the regulation small yellow panels. With the downturn in freight traffic, the yard here is being used to store rows of withdrawn brake vans, some clearly of considerable age. ***Brian Stephenson***

Above: 4-SUB 4114, another of the first ten 'all steel' units, has just arrived at Sevenoaks with a working from Holborn Viaduct via the Catford loop and Bat & Ball in about 1957. By this time SUBs were still prominent on former L.C.D.R. suburban routes, but South Eastern lines serving Charing Cross and Cannon Street were largely EPB-worked.
Chris Wilson Collection

Right: In clean ex-works condition, 2-NOL 1870 calls at Wandsworth Road with the 11.08 Victoria – London Bridge South London line service on 23 September 1951. At this time NOLs were frequently deputising for the increasingly unreliable 2-SL units (see page 136) on this line, although their bodywork was actually ten years older. ***J. H. Aston***

Commuters prepare to board as 4-CEP 7170 draws to a halt at Chatham with a morning Ramsgate – Victoria fast service in about 1966. 7170 was one of the later CEPs, built for phase 2 of the Kent Coast electrification, and differed in detail from earlier examples. Chatham station retains its L.C.D.R. buildings, footbridge and platform canopies, but the rather brutal 'slot-together' concrete fencing dates from the 1959 electrification when the outside loop lines were abolished to allow platform lengthening. ***Chris Wilson Collection***

The leading motor brake second and buffet car of 4-BEP 7017 are seen in close-up at Ashford, leading a Charing Cross – Margate service on 21 September 1966. Internally, the Kent Coast buffets had the same layout as those in the Hastings line 6-B diesel units, and customers were seated at tables with loose chairs. The trailer bogies of the phase 2 CEPs and BEPS were of the heavy cast-steel 'Commonwealth' type, fitted in an attempt to improve riding quality. ***Denis Ovenden/Colour Rail***

The driver looks out of his sliding cab window as 4-EPB unit 5193 prepares to depart from platform 10 at Victoria (Central side) with a suburban service to Epsom Downs via Selhurst on 11 April 1965. At this late date, the numerals on the roller blind are still of the large type, similar in size to the hook-on stencils of earlier stock, and a yellow warning panel is yet to be applied. To the left, a 4-LAV unit waits at platform 13 with a Brighton train. ***Brian Stephenson***

4-COR 3135 stands at Waterloo waiting to depart with a fast service to Portsmouth Harbour in September 1969. Typically, although motor brake second 11188 is clean and shiny, the rubbing plate of the prominent gangway is scuffed and dirty. ***Chris Wilson Collection***

3005
12
AIR FRANCE

Opposite: Seen from the Boutflower Road overbridge, 6-PUL 3005 curves to run parallel with the South Western main line on the approach to Clapham Junction with a morning Brighton - Victoria semi-fast service via Redhill in about 1965. The handsome motor coaches of these units had self-balancing drop-down windows which lowered about 6 inches. Unit 3005 was reformed as 6-COR 3050 in May 1966 and was finally withdrawn in September 1968. ***Brian Stephenson***

Above: 2-BIL 2079 leads a ten-car Victoria – Bognor Regis via Gatwick Airport stopping service passing South Croydon on a sunny afternoon in July 1969. The second unit of the five making up this service has gained full yellow ends wrapping around the cab corners. This train will call at platform 2 at Gatwick Airport, where the rear all-steel 2-HAL will detach. ***Brian Stephenson***

Left: Nicely framed by trees in this attractive west Surrey location, 2-BIL 2032 leads an all-steel 2-HAL between Woking and Brookwood on 3 June 1967, forming the Alton portion of a stopping service from Waterloo. At Woking, a Portsmouth and Southsea portion would have divided from this train. 2032 would later gain yellow ends before being withdrawn in June 1971.
Patrick Russell/Rail Archive Stephenson

Opposite: The SR was later than other BR Regions in generally adopting yellow warning panels on cab ends, but several different sizes and shapes were trialled. In this rare 1962 view 4-SUB 4378, given an experimental long and narrow 'Eastern Region' style panel, passes Crystal Palace with an empty stock working bound for Selhurst.
Brian Stephenson

4378
74

All-steel 4-SUB 4712 calls at Tulse Hill with a 'roundabout' service from Holborn Viaduct via Wimbledon, Sutton and West Croydon on 7 June 1958. As with many south London suburban stations in the immediate post-war years, a lick of paint was sorely needed. ***Chris Wilson Collection***

Opposite: 4-COR 3142 squeals around the curve into Fratton station leading a twelve-coach Portsmouth Harbour – Waterloo semi-fast service on Saturday 23 August 1969. Headcode '84' indicates that this train was routed via the Guildford 'New' line through Cobham. Livery is still green but the complete cab ends are yellow, a combination it carried between May 1967 and July 1970. ***John H. Bird/www.anistr.com***

3142
3142
84
NOTICE
PASSENGERS MUST
CROSS THE LINE
BY FOOTBRIDGE
DANGER

2-SL unit 1805 calls at Waddon Marsh Halt with the 14.51 West Croydon – Wimbledon service on 23 October 1954, on one of its last runs in public service. 1805 was converted in 1928 from two 1909-vintage A.C. motor coaches and retained the depressed roofs over the cabs where the collector bows had been. Also of interest, is the full width '2' stencil headcode. Close to central Croydon, Waddon Marsh Halt was built for the electrification of the route in 1930 and its environs included a gas works and power station, served by an extensive network of sidings. Not far away was the Tri-ang toy factory, also connected by a siding to this line. ***J. J. Smith/Bluebell Museum Archive***

New 'Brighton replacement' 4-CIG express unit 7313 stands at Victoria with an Eastbourne and Ore service during in about April 1965. The rounded cab ends of these units were made from glass-reinforced plastic, self-coloured green, incorporating recesses for the jumper cables. More important were the new B5S bogies and single centrally located motor coach, giving a much-improved ride in comparison with any previous S.R. electric stock. One of the 6-PUL units it will replace lurks in the shadows on the right. **Chris Wilson Collection**

Left: 2-NOL units 1826 and 1846 bask in the sun at Ore while waiting to return with a stopping service along the coast to Eastbourne and Brighton on 3 June 1958. Within a few weeks they will have been displaced from their coastal duties by 2-HAL units transferred from Medway services, and will then spend a short period on London suburban duties before being withdrawn. The underframes and bogies of both these units were re-used under new 2-EPB stock for the Windsor lines. Although Ore was the limit of electric working, conductor rails continued eastwards for a short distance to provide a headshunt for units entering or leaving the carriage shed here. ***Dr Terry Gough/The Transport Library***

Opposite: The low winter sun captures all the detail on 4-COR 3125, ex-works in British Rail blue, as it passes Wimbledon leading a COR+BUF+COR formation on an afternoon Waterloo – Portsmouth Harbour fast service in early March 1967. The immaculate full yellow ends will not remain clean for long. 3125 was the very first 'Nelson' unit to receive this livery, and this was possibly its first day in traffic following repainting. The photographer was standing on the Worple Road footbridge, always a popular location for train watching on the South Western main line. ***Brian Stephenson***

3125
3125
80

Unit 3121 leads a twelve-car COR+BUF+COR formation south of Horsham on a Victoria – Portsmouth/Bognor via Dorking service in about 1959. The end gangways of these units could oscillate wildly from side to side at speed, giving rise to another name given to this stock – 'belly wobblers'. Only the leading unit, forming the Portsmouth Harbour portion, is carrying roofboards. ***John Scrace***

2-HAL 2604 eases through West Norwood leading a Victoria – Brighton via Redhill stopping service on Tuesday 9 March 1965, diverted via Streatham Hill and Crystal Palace due to engineering work on the main line. The driver seems to be looking askance that anyone should want to photograph such a boring train! ***Brian Stephenson***

An inescapable fact of suburban railway operation is that much of the expensive equipment necessary to operate the peak hour service lies idle at other times. 2-BIL 2149, then less than twenty years old, is berthed at Three Bridges through the off-peak period on 9 October 1955. The wooden staff walkway has clearly been built to last. ***Dr Terry Gough/The Transport Library***

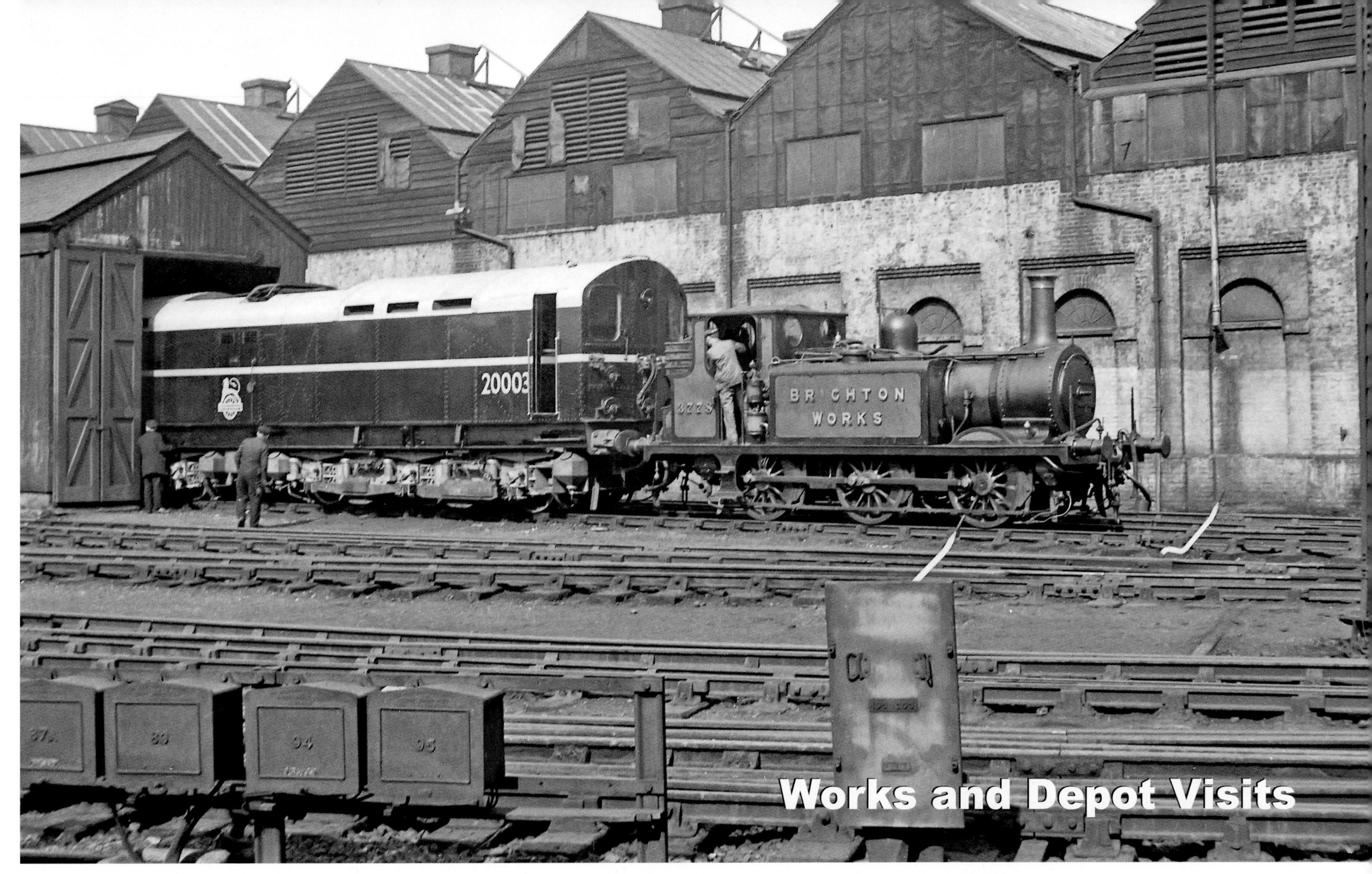

Works and Depot Visits

Following its first repaint, 'Hornby' 20003 is pulled out of the paint-shop at Brighton Works on 28 March 1950 by departmental Terrier 0-6-0T 377S. It was the first of the three to receive the new B.R. black livery specified for mixed traffic diesel and electric locomotives, based on the L.M.S. scheme for prototype diesels 10001 and 10002. The roof, lining band, frames, bogies and numbers were rather impractically painted silver, and the new 'cycling lion' emblem was displayed on the sides. The Southern Region wanted express green but was overruled for the time being. *Chris Wilson Collection*

Left: 'Hornby' 20001 is undergoing overhaul at Eastleigh during an organised Works visit on Wednesday 5 August 1959. While in undercoat its identity has been chalked on the front but in fact all three of these locomotives differed in external detail so this should not have been a problem. The wheelsets, of the Bulleid-Firth-Brown cast type, are in the foreground.
Dr Terry Gough/The Transport Library

Opposite: Five years later, sister locomotive 20002 has also visited Eastleigh Works and stands resplendent in a new coat of paint in August 1964. The light grey solebars were not very practical either and soon became coated in a layer of grime. ***Chris Wilson Collection***

Opposite: An unidentifiable S.R.-type EPB motor coach under repair is seen on the traverser at Lancing Carriage Works on 21 August 1963. Side panelling at the left-hand end has still to be replaced. The most likely candidate is 14350 from unit 5175, damaged in a converging collision at Orpington depot the previous month. ***Ian Nolan***

In 1958, Eastleigh Carriage Works was fully occupied building new electric units for the forthcoming Kent Coast electrification. However, on Saturday 31 May, the occasion of an organised visit, little of this activity was taking place. In the upper view 2-HAP vehicles are under construction. The leading vehicle is a B.R. Standard 60xx motor brake second whose bodywork has been painted and transfers applied, although the self-coloured glass-fibre doors have yet to be added. Behind are two 56xx unpainted driving trailer composites, built to Bulleid design on former 2-NOL underframes. To the right, unit 5606 has just been painted. The lower view shows 4-CEP vehicles in the later stages of body construction. A motor brake second is nearest, and doors have just been fitted. In the foreground is a pile of wooden shoebeams. ***Both: Stephenson Locomotive Society***

A new electric locomotive running maintenance shed, of somewhat utilitarian construction, was built at Stewarts Lane in 1959 to house both the type HA Bo-Bo and 'Hornby' Co-Co 'booster' locomotives. It was also the original base for the new type JA electro-diesels when they entered service and here E6001 in original condition is parked outside when brand new in April 1962. It was built in Eastleigh Carriage Works and is painted in dark green with round B.R. badges and an experimental yellow warning panel, later painted out. It is also fitted with coach-type self-contained oval buffers. A 2-HAP unit is berthed in the sidings behind. ***A. Baldwyn/Rail Archive Stephenson***

This July 1966 view shows 20003 inside Stewarts Lane electric locomotive shed, in exceptionally clean condition so it has probably been prepared for working a Pullman or Royal special. ***Chris Wilson Collection***

Nearly new 2-EPB 5722 passes Peckham Rye depot with a with a South London line working from Victoria to London Bridge on 17 February 1957. Another 2-EPB shows its cab outside the running shed and an all-steel 4-SUB is berthed behind. The line in the foreground leads to Tulse Hill. Peckham Rye depot was built for the 1909 South London line electrification and the high roofs of the sheds were necessary to clear the overhead wiring of the high tension 6700V 25Hz A.C. system used. The heavy overhaul shed in the background has a different roof due to wartime repairs. *R. C. Riley/The Transport Treasury*

Saloon-type 4-SUB 4689 is being given a good clean as it passes through the Stewarts Lane automatic carriage washer on 24 March 1966. The kinked guard irons in front of the leading wheels show that the motor bogie is of the 9ft-wheelbase 'Eastern' type, originally built in 1925 and recovered from a scrapped S.E.C.R.-bodied pre-war unit. ***Chris Wilson Collection***

Left: 4-SUB 4120, one of the first 'all-steel' units, also receives a thorough soaking as it goes through the washer at Lover's Walk, Brighton, in June 1969. The rather grubby cab end has, however, barely been wetted. It probably arrived on the coast coupled to a train of BIL and HAL units from London, to increase passenger capacity at a busy time. ***Colour Rail***

Opposite: Shortly after emerging into the light of day from Eastleigh Carriage Works, prototype JA electro-diesel E6001 tests its vacuum brake capability on a rake of Bulleid and B.R. steam stock at Barton Mill sidings, Basingstoke, in April 1962. The JA's were designed as versatile 'go anywhere' locomotives and used many standard E.M.U. components. Apart from their diesel capability to work away from the live rail, they were dual-braked, and their narrow bodies would fit down the restricted Tonbridge – Hastings line. They also had 27-wire control jumpers to work in multiple with any post-1951 electric stock.
David Brown Collection

Something New

PLATFORM
3
GENTLEMEN
7140
7140
S 61363
GUARD

Opposite: Brand new 4-CEP unit 7140 is parked in Dover Priory berthing siding on 17 May 1959, a month prior to the start of full Kent Coast phase 1 electric services on 15 June. These units were effectively a modernised version of the pre-war COR's to B.R. standard design parameters and with electro-pneumatic brakes. The driving cabs were simply standard coach ends with the necessary features, such as windows, jumper cables and headcode box, added. ***Colour Rail***

Up to thirty of these newly-delivered 4-CEP units were stored on the down line between Horsted Keynes and Ardingly prior to entry into service and in this view from the lineside near Ardingly, dated Sunday 24 May 1959, the line of units stretches almost as far as the eye can see towards Linwood tunnel. The nearest vehicle is trailer composite 73012 in unit 7120. ***J. J. Smith/Bluebell Museum Archive***

The row of stored CEP units as seen from the north end of Ardingly station, also on 25 May 1959, is headed by unit 7137. As the units were in warm storage, they were regularly taken off the front of the queue, given a test run on the Brighton line, and returned to the rear, reversing in the one electrified platform at Horsted Keynes. In the meantime, the queue was moved up. Prior to its use for storing new electric stock, this line had been used to store redundant steam stock and condemned wagons before that. ***J. J. Smith/Bluebell Museum Archive***

In immaculate external condition, new type HA 'booster' locomotive E5022 for the Kent Coast electrification is on display at the 'Modern Railway Travel' exhibition which took place in Battersea Wharf goods yard on 28-30 June 1959. The exhibition showcased new items of railway equipment then being introduced as the 1955 B.R. Modernisation Plan came on stream. ***J. H. Aston***

Seen from a passing train, a line of brand-new 4-CIG and 4-BIG Brighton replacement stock is stored in the sidings at Ford on 30 August 1965. Nearest the buffer stops is 4-BIG buffet unit 7033. In subsequent years these same sidings would play host to new 4-VEP stock and then successively to withdrawn 4-LAV, 6-COR, 2-BIL, 2-HAL and 4-COR units prior to stripping and being sent for scrap. ***John H. Bird/www.anistr.com***

Opposite: With the debris of steam operation still evident around it, production type JB electro-diesel E6037, built by English Electric at the Vulcan Foundry in Newton Le willows, is parked at Stewarts Lane on 10 September 1966, shortly after delivery. In the background is Inspection Saloon DS 70155, converted from a Maunsell 'Restriction 0' Hastings line corridor coach. ***John H. Bird/www.anistr.com***

DECCA
E6037

The first of the Kent Coast Motor Luggage Vans, 68001, has clearly just been delivered from Eastleigh Carriage Works when seen in rather untidy surroundings at Stewarts Lane in May 1959. The traction batteries, enabling them to work off the live rail for a short time on reduced power, are located under the hatches behind the leading cab door, and there was a charging point nearby outside Grosvenor Road carriage shed. The MLVs could also haul a small trailing load and were dual braked for this purpose. ***The Transport Treasury***

Bulleid's strange 4-DD units 4001 and 4002 approach Sidcup with an afternoon Dartford loop line service to Charing Cross in November 1949 when brand new. Headcode 40 indicates that they would travel direct from Hither Green to St John's, avoiding Lewisham. The idea of 'interlaced' upper and lower deck compartments was allegedly inspired by a pre-war Rome bus, described in an issue of 'Southern Railway Magazine'. This is quite possibly a publicity shot or taken on the first day of passenger service. ***David Brown Collection***

2-HAL 2699, in ex-works condition, stands at Victoria (Eastern) on Saturday 2 April 1949, waiting to depart with the 12.28 to Maidstone East. This was one of seven units ordered to replace war losses and had all-steel bodywork of Bullied design, similar to the suburban stock then in production. It has been outshoppped in post-war Southern Railway malachite green livery, and there is no evidence of B.R. ownership other than the small 's' prefix (for Southern Region) to the unit and coach numbers. The extra-large brake area held up to two tons (evenly distributed) and for this reason these units were dedicated to the Victoria – Gatwick Airport service from 1958. ***J. H. Aston***

Co-Co 'booster' electric locomotive 20003 stands under the shearlegs at Brighton shed when brand new in 1948. It too was outshopped in late Southern Railway lined malachite green, but with 'BRITISH RAILWAYS' on the sides. ***Wilfred Beckerlegge/Rail Archive Stephenson***

Above: 2-EPB 5701, the first Southern Region electric unit built to B.R. standard non-corridor design, poses for its portrait having just been outshopped from Eastleigh Carriage Works in December 1953. 79 units of this type were originally built, mainly for the Eastern Section 'ten car scheme' but also for single use on lightly used lines such as Wimbledon – West Croydon. Although superficially similar to the S.R.-bodied 4-EPBs also in production at the time, they were actually entirely different in detail. ***S.R. Official/David Brown Collection***

Left: The interior of one of the centre-gangway saloons of the prototype 2-EPB, 5701 when new in 1954. This basic design was adopted for all subsequent Southern electric non-corridor saloon vehicles of B.R. standard pattern, but the upholstery moquette shown was apparently unique to this particular unit. ***S.R. Official/David Brown Collection***

2-EPB 5671 stands outside Eastleigh Carriage Works when just completed on 18 November 1959, with driving trailer second leading. This was one of 24 such units constructed with new Bulleid-style bodywork on the reconditioned underframes and bogies of 2-NOL vehicles. They were the final units built with this bodywork design, after a production period of 14 years including SUB, EPB and HAP stock. They were also notable in being the first S.R. electric units with entirely open accommodation, although each coach was divided by a solid partition into two saloons. Although the doors with their toplights appeared absolutely standard, they were in fact moulded from glass reinforced plastic (fibreglass), self-coloured green. These units worked the Waterloo – Windsor/Weybridge service, dividing and combining at Staines. ***S.R. Official/David Brown Collection***

Above: A 'new' Isle of Wight seven-car formation, formed of 3-TIS unit 037 and 4-VEC 043, stands at Woking during a mainland test run down the South Western main line on 15 July 1966. The vehicles would later be taken over to the island one-by-one by low-loader on the Portsmouth – Fishbourne car ferry. ***John H. Bird/www.anistr.com***

Left: I.O.W. control trailer S38S, the first tube car to arrive on the island, pauses at Ryde St John's Road during a demonstration run to Shanklin on a very wet 25 September 1966. Hauled by Class O2, No.24 Calbourne the trip showed Ministry of Transport officials the difference in platform heights required for tube stock. The necessary compressed air supply to open and close the sliding doors and operate the brakes was provided from the Westinghouse pump of the locomotive.
David Brown Collection

4-CIG unit 7341, newly delivered in blue and grey livery from York Carriage Works, arrives at St. Denys with the 14.13 Bournemouth – Waterloo stopping service on 22 June 1970. These units were built to replace the 4-COR stock on the Portsmouth direct and Reading lines but had inferior seating to the earlier Brighton line units delivered five years previously. On the down line, an unidentified class 33 diesel waits for the road at the impressive signal gantry. ***John H. Bird/www.anistr.com***

Service Life Over

The unloved and life-expired 6-COR units saw only sporadic use through 1968, and their final runs in passenger service took place in early November. Following withdrawal, they were dumped at various points around the region, and here four of the ten are in store at Ford on 24 March 1969 as seen from the western end of the down platform. The units present are 3044, 3046, 3047 and 3049. These sidings had earlier held withdrawn 4-LAV units and, before that, brand new 4-CIG, BIG and VEP stock. The photographer later pictured these units from a passing train on the same day, just as 2-BIL 2101 approaches with a Portsmouth – Brighton service. Nearest is unit 3049, formed mainly from former 6-PUL 3015 but with two trailers from 6-PAN 3026. Motor coach 11029 is facing the camera. Close observation reveals that the roof-board brackets have been removed, necessary for their short summer visits to the Thanet main line in 1967 and 1968. 3049 had officially been withdrawn the previous 28 December and remained at Ford until the following September, after which it was moved to Selhurst for stripping and thence via Clapham Yard to the Micheldever carriage dump. Four vehicles were finally scrapped by Cashmore's at Newport, but the underframes of two trailers became flat wagons for transporting continuous welded rail.
Both: John H. Bird/www.anistr.com

2101
62
3049
PL

Left: Withdrawn trailer kitchen second 12618 from 4 RES unit 3071 is parked at Hither Green depot in use as a temporary 'shed on wheels' in about June 1964. The end gangway has been removed and its opening, together with a broken window, boarded up. It was dismantled on site later that year. These loss-making vehicles were withdrawn from passenger service on the Portsmouth line at the start of 1964 and were among the first coaches of S.R. express stock to go for scrap. ***The Lens of Sutton Association***

Below: Having recently arrived, three condemned 6-PUL Pullman Composite Cars and sundry other vehicles are being shunted at King's scrapyard, Wymondham, by D2018 in about March 1966. From 1964 withdrawn stock was sold to private scrap dealers, often after some time in store at Micheldever and elsewhere. Many of these merchants were, or had been, involved in the breaking-up of steam locomotives and, prior to that, shipping. Kings, based at Norwich, operated several sites in East Anglia. Much S.R. electric main line stock met its end at Wymondham, particularly steel bodied PUL & PAN motor coaches and the Pullman Composites. ***Dr. Ian C. Allen/The Transport Treasury***

This panoramic view of the eastern end of Micheldever sidings is dominated by the former ambulance train sheds built just prior to the start of World War Two. Laid out in the vast chalk pit originally excavated by the L.S.W.R. to provide hard-core for the construction of Southampton Docks, these sidings became the main Southern Region dumping ground for condemned, damaged or otherwise stored electric stock from about 1960. Withdrawn 7-TC trailer set 701, used on the Oxted line from 1963 until 1967, was present on 10 February 1969 prior to being disbanded. Although the former 2-BIL end coaches were then scrapped, all five 'six-a-side' centre vehicles saw further use in 4-SUB or EPB units. Running behind the sidings is the Bournemouth main line with Popham tunnel mouth just visible on the right. ***John H. Bird/www.anistr.com***

Left: Damaged stock unable to be moved far tended to end up at the buffer stops by the sheer chalk face adjacent to Popham tunnel. Such a vehicle was motor coach 14544 from 2-HAP 5624, which has clearly suffered significant collision damage and was eventually broken up on site in November 1967. During the 1960s and early '70s it was relatively easy, even for minors, to obtain a permit to wander unsupervised around the sidings at Micheldever. ***David Brown Collection***

Right Micheldever often held various departmental vehicles which were either temporarily or permanently out of use. S15 was another pair of 1925 'long-frame' suburban motor coaches retained after withdrawal from passenger service in 1959/60, this time as a test unit. Unlike similar de-icing units, few alterations appear to have been carried out other than the stripping of most external door and commode handles. No evidence of its usage has been unearthed and it spent the decade languishing uncared-for in various depots and berthing sidings. It did gain a yellow warning panel at some point but retained its original letter headcode stencils, the very last unit to do so; it is hoped that someone was foresighted enough to 'recover' them. This view dates from late 1969, at which point it has clearly been condemned.

David Brown Collection

The three vehicles of S.E.C.R.-bodied unit 4446 (formerly 1419) were having their bodywork dismantled at Lancing on 5 September 1951. The upper view shows trailer third (formerly composite) 9495 and the lower shows motor third brake 8263. These two views demonstrate how the work was done, entirely by hand using basic tools and brute force. Note how the wooden roof has been sawn through to make sections of convenient length. Only when completely dismantled were the component parts consigned to the bonfires. In the days before health and safety legislation the workmen concerned had, no doubt, to take particular care to avoid broken glass and rusty nails. The standard 62ft steel underframes and bogies, appreciably younger than the superstructure, were then reconditioned and given new steel bodies – in this case to form saloon-bodied 4-EPB vehicles. ***J. H. Aston***

For ten years from around 1954, these sidings at Newhaven Town were used to dismantle withdrawn suburban electric units and sundry other vehicles, again mainly by hand. Photographs during this period are understandably rare but on Easter Sunday 1959, a day when clearly no activity was taking place, four 2-NOL vehicles are awaiting their fate. Their bodywork, of L.S.W.R. origin, was now more than half a century old. These were among the last timber-bodied vehicles to be broken up here, their steel underframes being reused under 2-EPB stock for the Windsor line. ***J. J. Smith/Bluebell Museum Archive***

Opposite: 2-BIL unit 2133 was one of the class formed with an all-steel 2-HAL type driving trailer composite following accident damage. Following withdrawal in June 1971, it spent some time stored in sidings near Feltham, where it was photographed in the late autumn of 1971 in full view of passengers from passing trains. As was usual, the doors had been removed from the steel-bodied vehicle as spares for possible further use in similar 4-SUB and EPB stock which remained in service, but the apertures have been barred with wooden strips. 2133 was scrapped by Kings at Wymondham in December 1971. ***David Brown Collection***

Right: From the late 1940s onwards, there were many dumping points around the Southern Region where redundant stock was parked awaiting disposal, mostly outside the electrified area. Among the most obscure was the disused spur at Worthy Down, built during World War Two to connect the erstwhile G.W.R. Didcot, Newbury and Southampton line to the Bournemouth main line north of Winchester. In 1961-62 this was used to store vehicles from the '4326' series 4-SUB units, built new in 1925 and the last of the first-generation suburban stock to be withdrawn. Motor coach 8469 from unit 4352 was present there in December 1961 and was scrapped at Newhaven the following month. As noted previously, some vehicles of this class were converted for an extended life as de-icing units or for other departmental purposes. *Peter Swift*

This general view of Micheldever sidings, looking north-east at track level, was photographed on 12 April 1971 and shows various items of withdrawn electric stock in residence. In the foreground is 2-HAL 2616, flanked by 4-BUF 3076 on the left the damaged 2-BIL on the right is thought to be 2103 which had been in collision with 4-SUBs 4717 & 4703 at Wimbledon Park the previous November. The proximity of the Bournemouth main line on the far left is clear from 4-TC 424 speeding past with a semi-fast train (headcode 92) from Waterloo. In the background the former ambulance train shed is being dismantled. ***John Medley/Rail Photoprints***